Mel Bay Presents

Celtic Auto

35 Celtic tunes arranged for all standard
Autoharps using notation and tablature

by Karen Mueller

GW01424186

CD Contents

1 Scotland the Brave [1:19]	13 Gavotte de Scrignac [:31]	25 Blarney Pilgrim [1:12] *CLA*
2 Red Haired Boy [1:10]	14 Britches Full of Stitches [:41] *SP*	26 Morrison's Jig [1:00]
3 Miss McLeod's Reel [1:07] *SP*	15 John Ryan's Polka [:54]	27 Merrily Kiss the Quaker [1:12] *CLA*
4 Flowers of Edinburgh [1:12]	16 Farewell to Whiskey [1:21]	28 The Star Above the Garter [:50] *SP*
5 Julia Delaney [1:17]	17 All Through the Night [:54]	29 Hardiman the Fiddler [:42] *STICE Powi*
6 Maid Behind the Bar [1:11]	18 Arran Boat Song [:57] *CLA*	30 The Butterfly [:58]
7 Miss Thornton's Reel [1:07]	19 Skye Boat Song [1:46]	31 Eleanor Plunkett [:52] *SP*
8 The Musical Priest [1:03]	20 Star of the County Down [1:22]	32 Carolan's Draught [2:13]
9 Walker Street [1:30]	21 Sonny's Mazurka [1:01]	33 Sheebeg Sheemor [1:42]
10 Star of Munster [1:19]	22 Ship in Full Sail [:51] *CLA*	34 Morgan Magan [2:06]
11 Harvest Home [1:23]	23 Kesh Jig [:54]	35 Captain O'Kane [1:11]
12 Rights of Man [1:25]	24 Larry O'Gaff [:57]	

1 2 3 4 5 6 7 8 9 0

MEL BAY ®

Visit us on the Web at http://www.melbay.com — E-mail us at email@melbay.com

The Celtic Autoharp

The author wishes to thank the following for their support, tunes and advice: William Bay, Maddie MacNeil, Dick Hensold, Dr. Sue, Jane Fallander and Newgrange. Extra special thanks to Janita Baker for her computer wizardry, diligence and sense of humor while making this book come to life on the page. Thanks also to my students for feedback on the arrangements.

May these tunes inspire more Autoharpers to join in sessions everywhere!

Table of Contents

Introduction

Welcome to *The Celtic Autoharp*! In this book you will find 35 tunes representing ten different styles from four Celtic countries or regions: Ireland, Scotland, Wales and Brittany (France). The majority of the pieces are dance tunes such as jigs and reels, which are popular at Irish sessions— informal music gatherings found in pubs, community halls and homes everywhere. The Autoharp is a relative new-comer to Celtic music, joining the fiddle, flute, accordion, bagpipes and others. Legend has it that the harp was the original instrument of Ireland, and the Autoharp bears more than a passing resemblance to the larger harp. Thus it is natural to include a section of tunes written by harpist Turlough O'Carolan, as well as other slow airs.

The Autoharp also produces a sound similar to a guitar, in both melodic fingerpicking and rhythmic accompaniment. When you listen to Celtic recordings, pay attention to the rhythm part behind the melody and work to develop your own backup style. Sample rhythm patterns are given at the end of this introduction. Learning backup will allow you to play with others even if you haven't mastered the melody up to speed yet. Also listen to the *pulse* of the music, the rhythmic quality found in the phrasing. This is especially evident when a group is playing together in the traditional unison manner, with everyone playing melody. Since it is impossible to convey this feeling in written music and tablature, it is essential to listen closely to recordings and performances at every opportunity and imitate what you hear. For this reason, using this book's companion recording is highly recommended. Additional resources for recordings are found at the back.

The level of this book would be considered intermediate to advanced. Some of the tunes are simpler and more familiar, such as *Scotland the Brave*, the first tune in the book. Please note, however, that the book is arranged by tune type, not by level of difficulty. The tablature used here is the most thorough means of describing what each hand is doing in order to play the pieces on the Autoharp. Becky Blackley, former editor of *Autoharpoholic* magazine (now out of print), developed the system. An explanation of the tablature symbols follows. It is assumed that a player is already familiar with the instrument and with melody picking technique in general, though an experienced musician from another instrument could most likely work through the arrangements using the tablature and the companion recording.

Besides a tuned Autoharp, the only other tools recommended are a plastic thumb pick and two or three fingerpicks, either metal or plastic. Other helpful equipment would include a metronome and a music stand. Because you're holding the instrument upright, you may wish to try using a strap to stabilize and possibly raise the Autoharp to a more comfortable height. Any instrument repair shop could install the strap buttons for you, one by the #36 (highest) tuning pin, and the other between the chord bars and the string anchor plate by string #1 (bass). These both go on the instrument's face, fairly close to the edge, screwed into the pinblock.

All of the pieces in this book have been arranged so that they are playable on any standard 15 or 21 bar chromatic Autoharp; no special tunings or chords are required. (If you play a 12 bar instrument, you will need a D major chord. You can create one from your D7 chord by plugging up the spaces for the C strings with some replacement felt.) Some pieces will indicate that the key of a tune has been changed to make it playable on a standard Autoharp. In these cases, the traditional key is noted, and will always be just one key higher than the key shown. To transpose the tune to its regular key, simply raise all notes and chord names by one whole step. This will be the next letter in the musical alphabet (A through G), sometimes including a sharp (see Basic Music Notation page that follows). For example, to change *The Musical Priest* from A minor to its traditional key of B minor, all the Am chords become Bm, all the G chords go up to A, and so forth. The right-hand movements remain the same, just played a bit higher. If you plan to play with others and go to sessions, it is imperative to play in the traditional keys.

In order to play in these other keys you'll need to modify your Autoharp by adding new chord bars or changing some of your current ones. Space does not permit a detailed explanation of this procedure, but you may consult the resources at the back of the book for further information. Regardless of which keys you use, it is helpful to rearrange your chord bars to make certain reaches easier. Players develop their own personal favorite chord bar arrangements after a while, but here are two simple suggestions. First, for a 15 bar instrument, move the D major and the A7 chords down closer to the G major. These three belong together in the key of D major, and the D chord is used in the key of G as well. You'll need to shuffle around the other chords in that row, possibly requiring some compromises; try different configurations to find the way that best suits your own playing.

The second suggestion, for 21 bar instruments, is to shift the position of the rows as they relate to each other. The original arrangement situates the major row first, the sevenths in the middle, and the minor chords in the last row (bass side). This makes the reach between the majors and the minors unnecessarily long and awkward. If we move the major row to the middle, with the minors in the first row, and the sevenths at the bass side, the reach is much easier. Carefully remove the plastic chord bar cover, and lift out the third bar from the left (A-flat) and put it aside. Move the second bar over to the third slot, and the first bar to the second. Return the third bar to the open first slot, then shift the white name buttons to their new positions. Repeat this process for the remaining bars, working three at a time. When you replace the cover you should see a shift in the rows as described above. It is a good idea to write down the original order of the bars before you begin, in case you decide to change the arrangement back, or things get disrupted as you're working.

Occasionally you may find it more convenient to use the seventh chord instead of the major of the same name. This substitution is fine as long as the chord is the "five" chord in the key; for example, in the key of G you may prefer to use the D7 instead of the D major as written. These are the only types of chords that are interchangeable. Be extra careful to pick the melody note cleanly, as the seventh chords include an extra note situated very near to another note in the chord. Sevenths typically aren't heard much in Celtic music and are thus sparsely used here.

Notes on the Tunes

The pieces in this book are presented by type and time signature, starting with 4/4 time. This rhythm is the most familiar, having a feeling as if one were walking—*left, right, left, right*—while counting *1, 2, 3, 4*. The first tune, *Scotland the Brave*, is a well known Scottish bagpipe **march** which exemplifies this sense of walking. The next section, the **reels**, begins with three tunes played frequently in American repertoires: *Red Haired Boy* (also called *The Little Beggarman*), *Miss McLeod's Reel* (known as *Hop High Ladies* in America) and *Flowers of Edinburgh*. Reels can be played emphasizing beats 1 and 3 (especially the Scottish tunes) or accenting the off-beat—beats 2 and 4—found more commonly in Irish music. Final tempos, taken from a metronome marking beats 1 and 3, can range from around 88 up to 138. Always remember to play slowly and evenly when learning a new tune, increasing speed gradually. Also, always observe the repeat signs; most of these tunes are played in the form AABB. A *coda* such as that found at the end of *Miss McLeod's Reel* is reserved for the conclusion of the tune.

Two **hornpipes** follow the reels. Hornpipes are similar to reels but have a distinctive rhythm and bouncy feeling. Note that although written in dotted notation, the count of each pair of eighth notes is "**1** (*e*) **&**" or "**1** (*2*) *3*" instead of "**1** (*e &*) **uh**", the regular dotted count. Hornpipes are normally played in this three-count, though they may be written in dotted or non-dotted eighth note form. They're usually played a bit slower than reels. The next tunes, the **gavotte** and the **polkas**, are lively and quick. Try the polkas together in a medley.

This brings us to a group of slower tunes, starting with *Farewell to Whiskey*, a **lament** attributed to Scottish composer and violinist Niel Gow (1727-1807). Tempo: no faster than 88, counting all beats. The next section combines **airs and songs**; airs are considered songs without words. *All Through the Night*, a lovely Welsh lullaby, is written here as an instrumental solo using an arpeggio picking pattern. Practice this right hand pattern (found on the tablature staff, first measure) until familiar: *pinch-index-thumb-index* to the count "1 & 2 &". Then follow the tablature carefully, using the pattern to play melody and fills. One of the best known Irish songs is *Star of the County Down*, presented here as an instrumental with words given at the end. Strum the backup chords when singing, and look for additional verses in folk song books. *Sonny's Mazurka* is a dance tune in 3/4 time that uses the same dotted rhythm as the hornpipes. Its tempo is moderate, faster than the airs.

The **jigs** (6/8), **slides** (12/8) and **slip jigs** (9/8) share the rhythmic feeling of a three-count. The eighth notes are frequently grouped together three at a time; a jig is counted "**1** 2 3 **4** 5 6" with the accent on beats one and four. To maintain these accents, follow the right hand pattern in the tablature carefully. These lilting tunes often sound the most characteristically "Irish" to listeners (though there are Scottish jigs as well). There will be little difference between the jigs and the slides other than the length of each measure. Try a tempo between 96 and 120, with the clicks marking beats 1 and 4. The slip jigs have a different feeling, a kind of jazz beat, and sound good played a bit slower.

The book ends with five pieces by the prolific Irish harpist **Turlough O'Carolan** (1670-1738). These tunes range from the slow, reflective air *Eleanor Plunkett* to the classical-sounding *Carolan's Draught*. O'Carolan compositions are often favorites among Autoharpers. Enjoy!

Explanation of Tablature

The music written in this book has this general form:

- The top staff is standard music notation and the bottom staff is Autoharp tablature.
- The line of upper case letters between the two staffs indicates the chord bars to be depressed with the left hand. A slash (/) means repeat the previous chord.
- To play rhythm accompaniment use the chords located above the top staff (suggested rhythm patterns follow). Chords in parentheses are optional substitutions.

Symbols on the tablature staff indicate these right-hand movements:

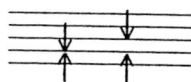

A **pinch** between the thumb and middle finger. This is the main melody-playing stroke. The middle finger plays the melody note. Always corresponds to the note indicated on the staff (examples—the notes *G* and *A*). Does not refer to width of stroke.

A **thumb strum** in the lower or middle octave, from lower strings to higher.

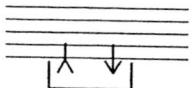

A **rhythm fill** beginning with a **thumb strum** and followed by a **middle finger brush** from higher strings to lower in a total of one beat of time (count "*one and*").

An **index finger pluck** of a single melody note, again coordinating with note indicated on staff (examples—the notes *B* and *A*).

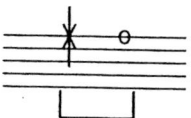

A **pinch stroke** followed by an **index finger pluck** in a total of one beat of time (count "*one and*").

A **thumb stroke** followed by an **index finger pluck**, again in a total of one beat of time (count "*one and*").

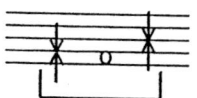

In a jig or slide, a group of three eighth notes, each note receiving one beat (count "*one two three*"). In 4/4 time, when the number 3 appears at the bottom of the bracket, this is a triplet (total time of one beat—count "*one and uh*").

A **hold** after a note or chord strum. May be either one beat in length or one-half beat, depending on the type of tune and the context.

Basic Music Notation

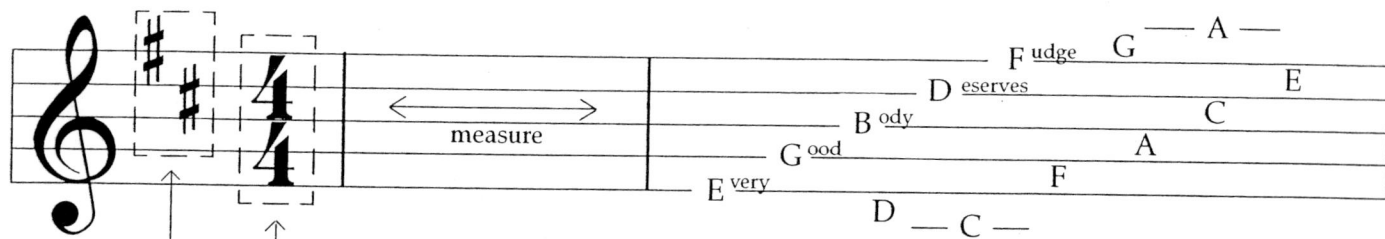

Key Signature: the number of sharps or flats denotes the key; they are written in the position of the note(s) to be affected.

Treble Clef Symbol

Time Signature: the top number designates the number of beats in a measure; the bottom number designates the type of note receiving one beat. For example, in a measure of **4/4** time, there are four beats to a measure and a quarter note gets one beat. In a measure of **6/8** time, there are six beats to a measure and an eighth note gets one beat.

Note Values

The length for which notes are held is usually associated with 4/4 time. However, an 8 on the bottom line of the time signature changes the value of the notes, as shown in the table at left.

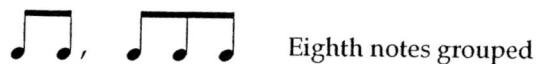

		Time Signature:	$4/4$	$6/8$
			Beats	
𝅝	whole note		4	—
𝅗𝅥	half note		2	4
𝅗𝅥.	dotted half		3	6
𝅘𝅥	quarter note		1	2
𝅘𝅥.	dotted quarter		$1 \ 1/2$	3
𝅘𝅥𝅮	eighth note		$1/2$	1
𝅘𝅥𝅯	sixteenth note		$1/4$	$1/2$

Eighth notes grouped

Sixteenth notes grouped

Half step: from one black or white key to the next [ex: C to C#, E to F]
Whole step: two half steps [ex: C to D, E to F#]

♯ = sharp: half step higher

♭ = flat: half step lower

♮ = natural: ♯ or ♭ is cancelled

KEYBOARD

| C# | D# | | F# | G# | A# | } same notes, different names |
| Db | Eb | | Gb | Ab | Bb | |

C D E F G A B C D E F G A B C D E F G A B

Playing Accompaniment

Also called rhythm or backup playing, accompaniment involves choosing a strumming pattern which fits the time signature of the piece, then using only the chords found above the top staff. Play the pattern for the number of measures (or partial measures) shown for a chord until the next chord is given. These chords will usually correspond to the melody chords (between the music and TAB staffs), but not always.

Here are some patterns in each time signature to get you started. The numbers below each example give its count. Accent the beat that appears in bold. To learn a new pattern, depress any chord bar and repeat the pattern until it feels comfortable; then plug it in to a tune. Getting familiar with the backup chords of a piece gives a good overview of the tune, and is important when playing with other lead (melody) instruments.

reels, marches, polkas

polkas (faster)

airs, slow tunes, waltzes, mazurkas

Captain O' Kane

Any of the 3/4 patterns played twice per measure

jigs

slip jigs

slides

Any 6/8 jig pattern played twice per measure

9

Scotland the Brave

Key: G

Red Haired Boy
(Little Beggarman)

Key: G
Trad. Key: A

Irish Reel

Miss McLeod's Reel

Key: G

Flowers of Edinburgh

Key: F
Trad. Key: G

Scottish Reel

Julia Delaney

Key: Dm

The Maid Behind the Bar

Key: C
Trad. Key: D

Miss Thornton's Reel

Key: G

Irish

The Musical Priest

Key: Am
Trad. Key: Bm

Irish Reel

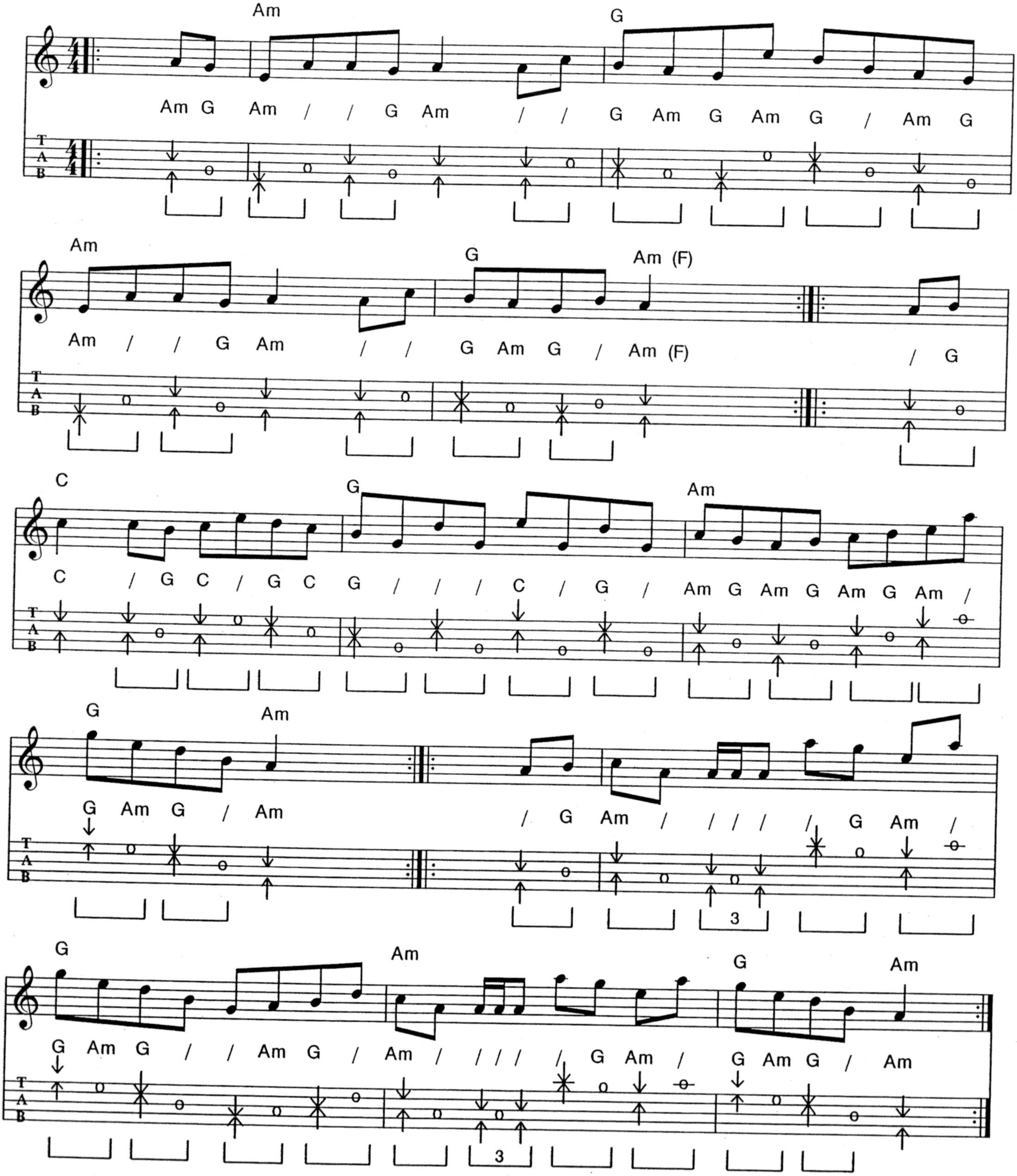

Walker Street

Key: C
Trad. Key: G or D

Scottish Reel

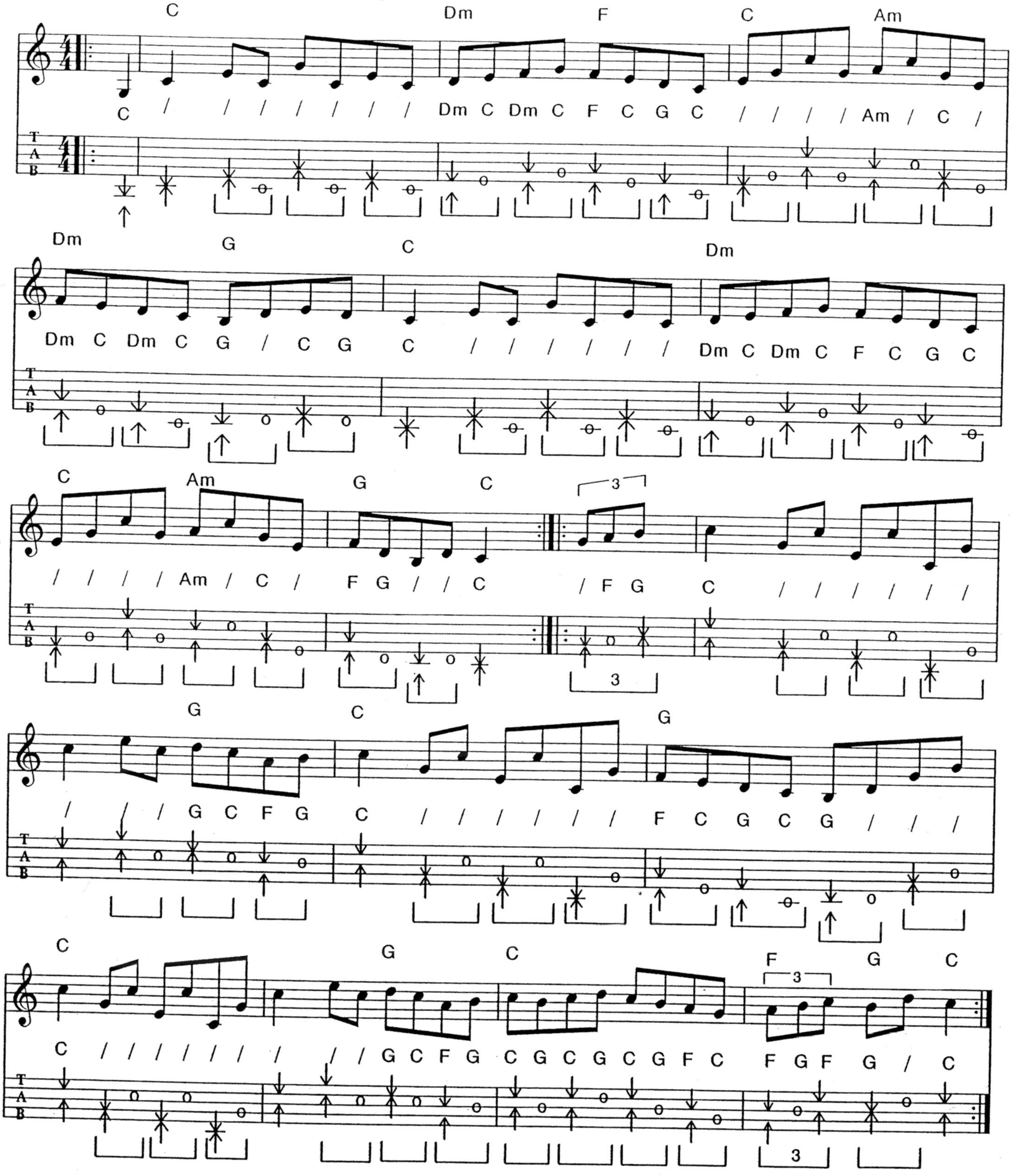

The Star of Munster

Key: Am

Irish Reel

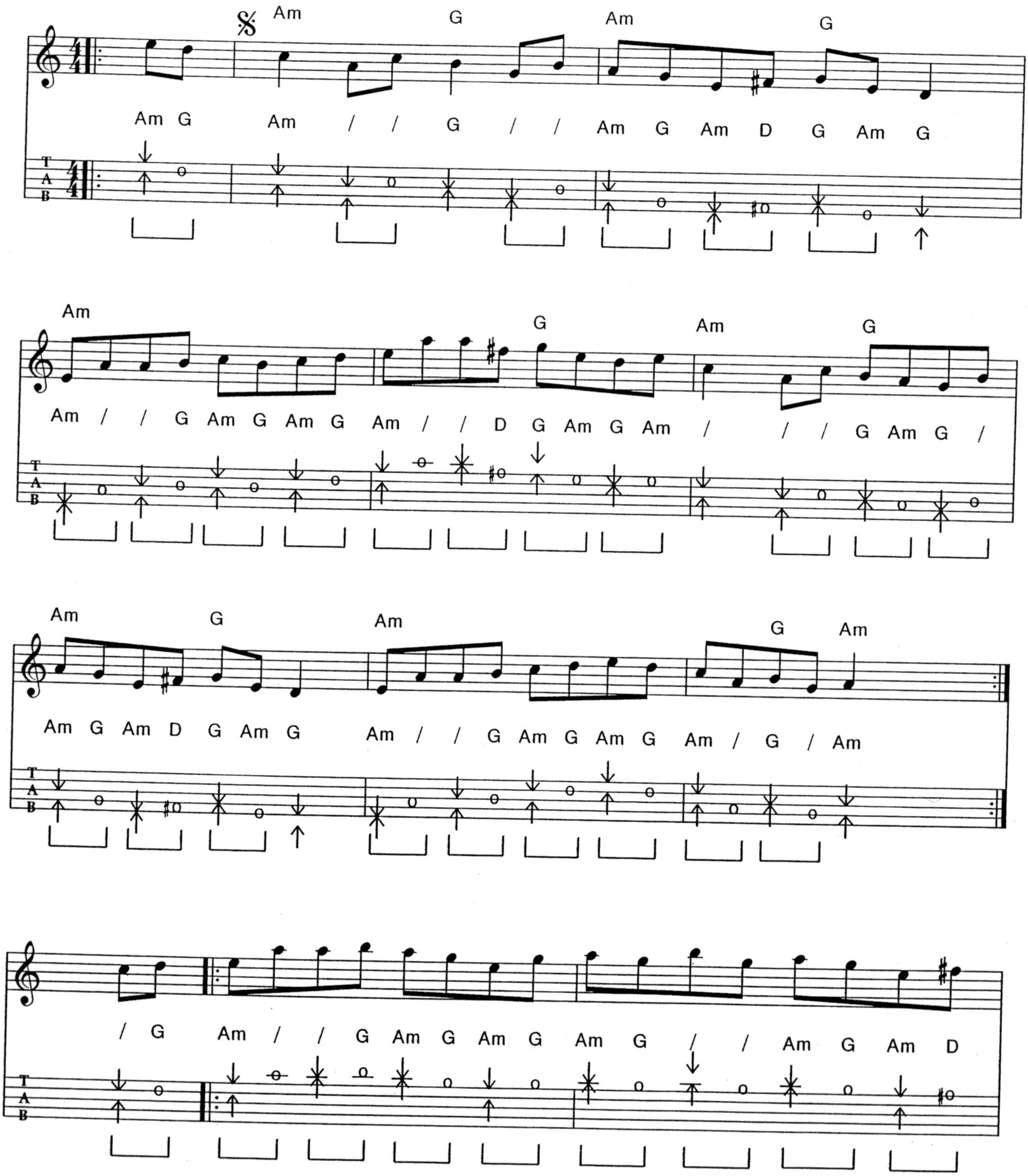

[The coda is played at the conclusion of the tune only. To return to part A, omit the first two pickup notes.]

Harvest Home

Key: D

Irish Hornpipe

Rights of Man

Key: Dm

Trad. Key: Em

Irish Hornpipe

Gavotte de Scrignac

Key: G

Trad. Key: A

Breton

Britches Full of Stitches

Key: G

Trad. Key: G or A

John Ryan's Polka

Key: C
Trad. Key: D

Irish

Farewell to Whiskey

Key: F
Trad. Key: G

Scottish
Niel Gow

All Through the Night

(Ar Hyd y Nos)

Key: C

Welsh

Arran Boat Song

Key: Dm
Trad. Key: Em

Scottish

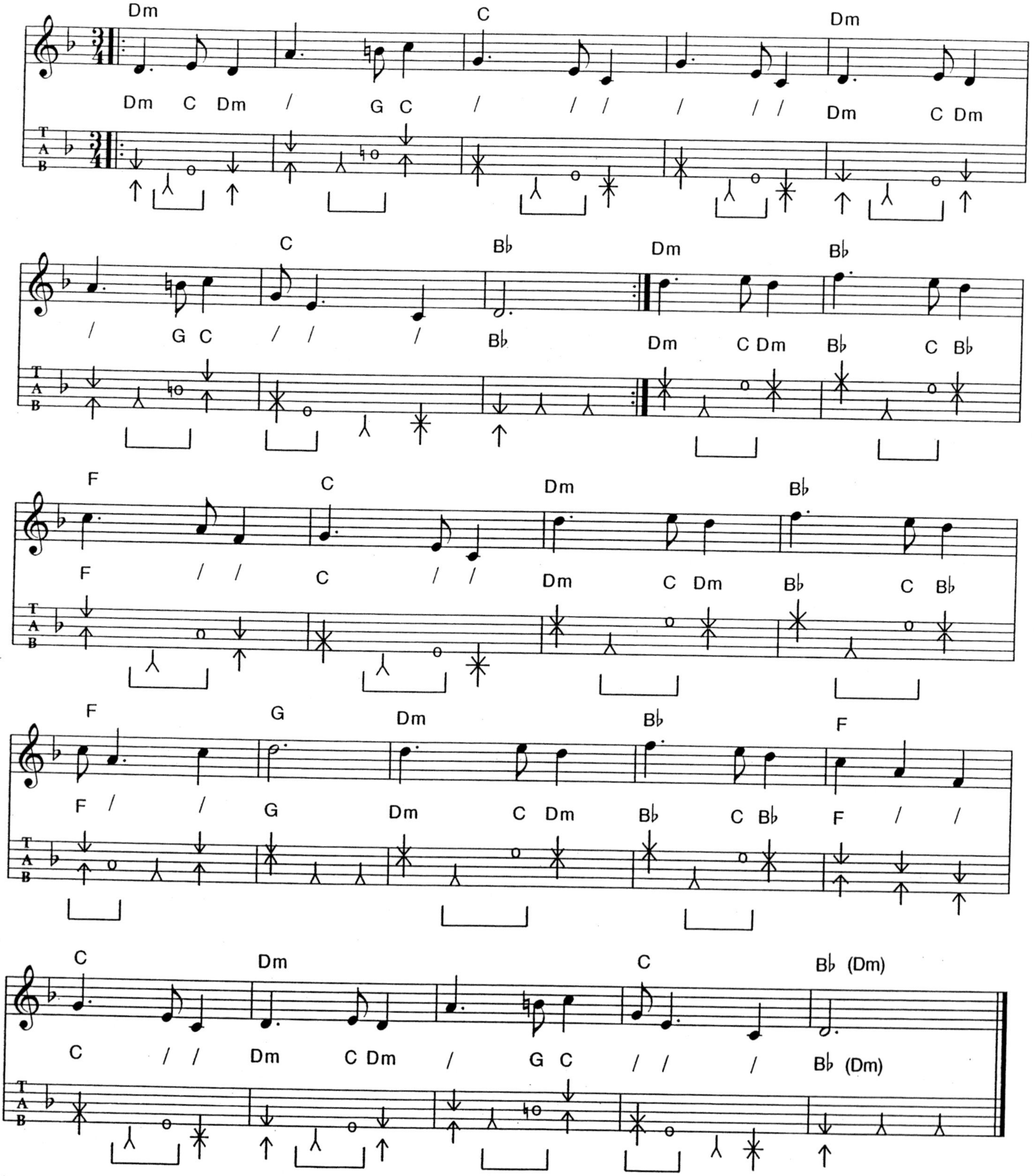

Skye Boat Song

Key: C
Trad. Key: D

Scottish

Star of the County Down

Key: Am

Irish Air and Song

VERSE (*tune: parts A & B₁*)

Near to Banbridge town in the County Down,
One morning last July,
Down a boreen green came a sweet colleen,
And she smiled as she passed me by.
She looked so neat from her two white feet
To the sheen of her nut brown hair,
Such a coaxing elf, I'd to shake myself,
To make sure I was really there

VERSE

At the harvest fair she'll be surely there,
So I'll dress in my Sunday clothes,
And I'll try sheep's eyes and deludtherin lies
On the heart of the nut brown Rose.
No pipe I'll smoke, no horse I'll yoke
Tho' my plow with rust turn brown,
Till a smiling bride by my own fireside
Sits the Star of the County Down.

CHORUS (*tune: B₂*)

From Bantry Bay up to Derry Quay,
And from Galway to Dublin Town,
No maid I've seen like the brown colleen
That I met in the County Down.

Sonny's Mazurka

Key: D

Irish

Ship in Full Sail

Key: G

Irish Jig

Kesh Jig

Key: G

Irish Jig

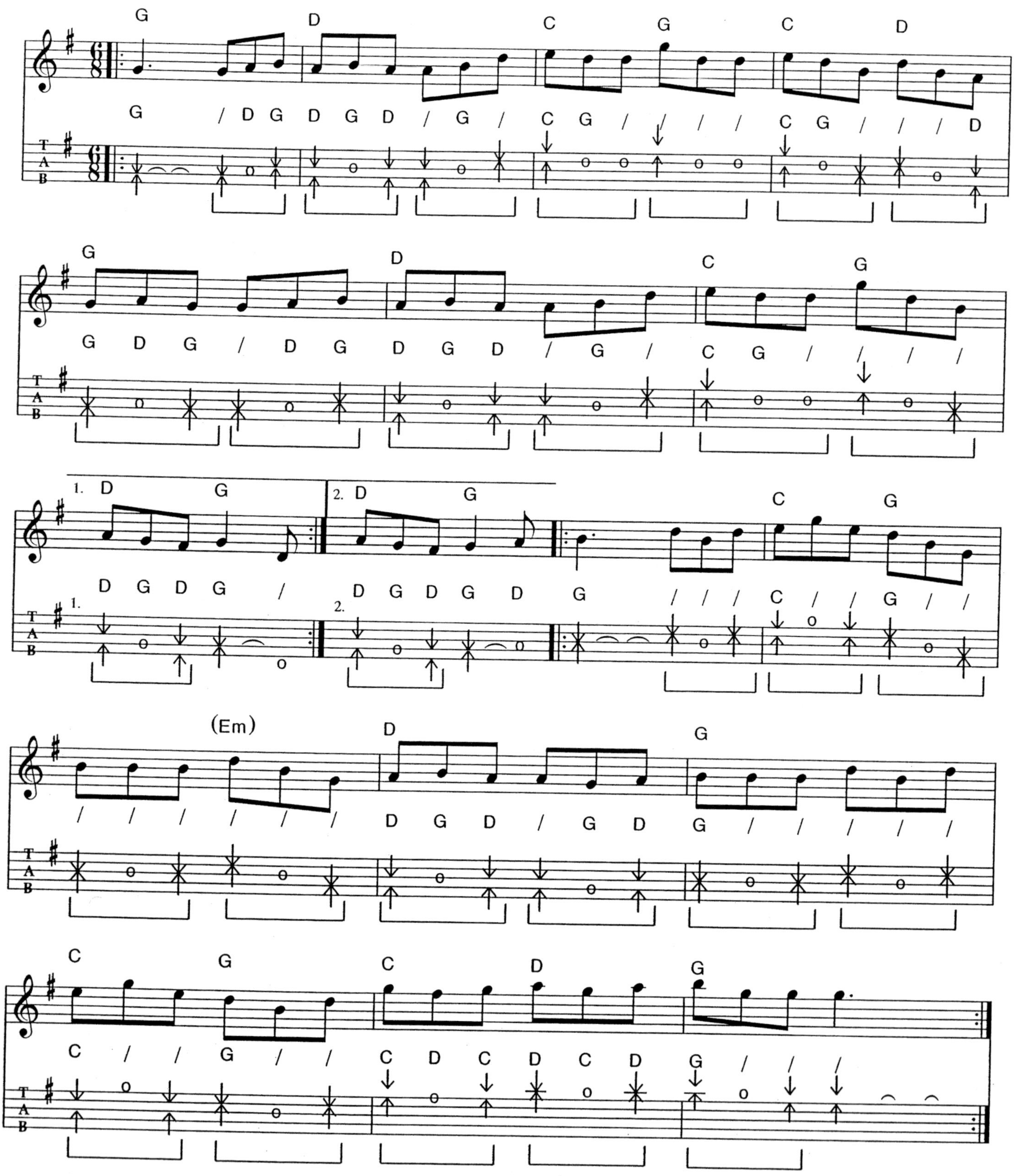

Larry O'Gaff

Key: G

Irish Jig

The Blarney Pilgrim

Key: G

Irish Jig

1. G
2. G
D G
G C G /
G D G / D G
D / / G / /
T A B
D G
D
D G D G C G D G D G C G D G C G
D G D G
D / / G / / D G D G C G D G D G C G C G /

Morrison's Jig

Key: Dm
Trad. Key: Em

C Dm C
F C F C G C Dm / / C Dm / C Dm / C Dm C
T A B
Dm C F
Dm / / C Dm / C / / / Dm C F / / C G
T A B
C F G C
C G C F / G C G C / F C F C G C
T A B
Coda
Dm
Dm
T A B

Merrily Kiss the Quaker

Key: G

Irish Slide

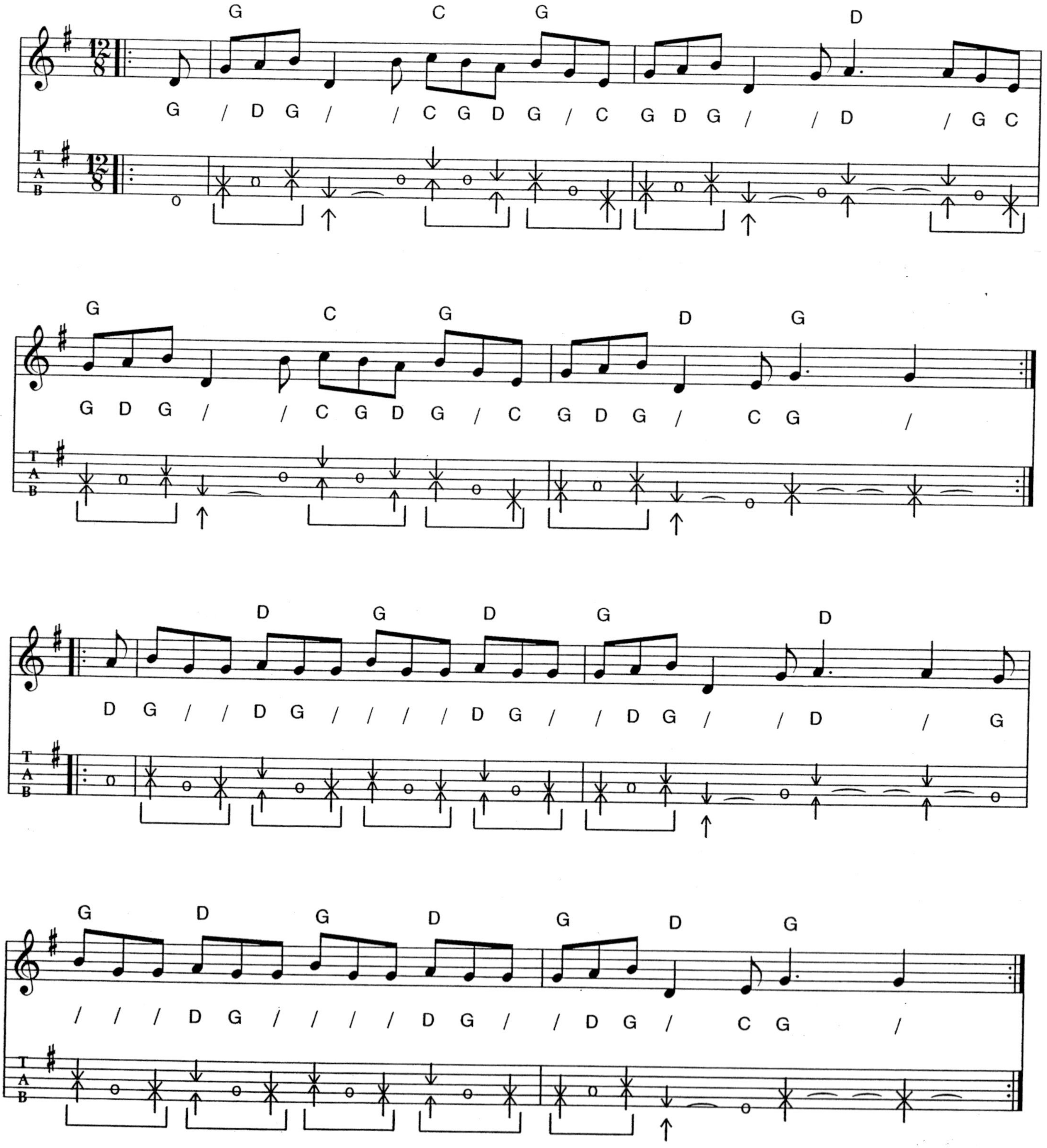

The Star Above the Garter

Key: G

Hardiman the Fiddler

Key: D

Irish Slip Jig

The Butterfly

Key: Dm
Trad. Key: Em

Irish Slip Jig

Eleanor Plunkett

Key: F
Trad. Key: G

Irish
Turlough O'Carolan

Carolan's Draught

Key: F
Trad. Key: G

Irish
Turlough O'Carolan

Sheebeg Sheemor

Irish
Turlough O'Carolan

Key: D

Morgan Magan

Key: G

G / / C D G / / C G / / / C G
C D G C G
C G C G D C G D G C G / C / G /
Am G D C
Am G Am G / D / / G D C / / D C / / /
D G C
D / / / C D C / D / G C G / / / C G C G
D G D 1. G 2. G
C G D G D G D / G / D G D / G / / C G
1. 2.

Captain O' Kane

Key: Dm
Trad. Key: Em
Slowly

Irish
Turlough O'Carolan

Alphabetical Index of Tunes

About the Author

Karen Mueller is a professional Autoharp performer and instructor specializing in Celtic and American music. The press has called her "one of the world's top Autoharp players" and "a true virtuoso." Winner of the 1986 International Autoharp Championship in Winfield, Kansas, Karen has traveled throughout the US and to Ireland, performing and joining in traditional music sessions with the Autoharp. Her other instruments include guitar, mandolin, bouzouki and mountain dulcimer. In addition to performing, Karen offers instructional workshops and private lessons to players of all levels. She has released several recordings and books, including the CD *Clarity*, and *The Autoharp Gourmet* book and tape. These and more are available through her Internet Web page and the vendors listed below. She resides in Minneapolis, Minnesota, where she is an instructor at West Bank School of Music and Homestead Pickin' Parlor.

Additional Resources

Autoharp Quarterly: Stonehill Productions, P.O. Box 336 / New Manchester, WV 26056
Autoharp Clearinghouse: Eileen Roys, Publisher. P.O. Box 398 / Chester, MD 21619
Autoharpoholic: Out of print; back issues available bound as *The Care and Feeding of the Autoharp* by Becky Blackley, through Elderly Instruments (see below)
Internet: The Autoharp Page (links to Karen Mueller's page) and Cyberpluckers mailing list

Celtic Tune Books and Record Labels

O'Neill's Music of Ireland, Oak or Mel Bay Publications
The Complete Works of Turlough O'Carolan, Ossian Publications
The Gow Collection of Scottish Dance Music, Oak Publications
The Fiddler's Fakebook, by David Brody, Oak Publications (contains a variety of styles)
Mel Bay's Irish Session Tune Book, by Cari Fuchs, Mel Bay Publications
Labels most easily found in the US: Green Linnet and Shanachie. These include such artists as Kevin Burke, Eileen Ivers, Bothy Band, Altan, Solas, Boys of the Lough, Silly Wizard.
Internet: Ceolas Celtic Web site—extensive source of tunes and resources

Mail-Order Retailers: Recordings, Books, Instruments & Accessories

Homestead Pickin' Parlor: 6625 Penn Ave. S. / Richfield, MN 55423 800/497-3655
Elderly Instruments: P.O. Box 14210 / Lansing, MI 48901 517/372-7890
Lark in the Morning: P.O. Box 1176 / Mendocino, CA 95460 707/964-5569
Andy's Front Hall: P.O. Box 307 / Voorheesville, NY 12186 518/765-4193